DINOSAUR ACTIVITY BOOK FOR KIDS

THIS BOOK BELONGS TO

_____

DINOSAUR

ACTIVITY BOOK
FOR KIDS

70 ACTIVITIES INCLUDING COLORING, DOT-TO-DOTS & SPOT THE DIFFERENCE

Lauren Thompson

Illustrated by
Sara Lynn Cramb

ROCKRIDGE
PRESS

For general information on our other products and services or to obtain technical support, please contact our Customer Care Department within the United States at (866) 744-2665, or outside the United States at (510) 253-0500.

Rockridge Press publishes its books in a variety of electronic and print formats. Some content that appears in print may not be available in electronic books, and vice versa.

TRADEMARKS: Rockridge Press and the Rockridge Press logo are trademarks or registered trademarks of Callisto Media Inc. and/or its affiliates, in the United States and other countries, and may not be used without written permission. All other trademarks are the property of their respective owners. Rockridge Press is not associated with any product or vendor mentioned in this book.

Interior and Cover Designer: Erin Yeung
Art Producer: Janice Ackerman
Editor: Annie Choi
Production Editor: Mia Moran

Illustrations © 2020 Sara Lynn Cramb

ISBN: Print 978-1-64739-822-4

R0

DRAW A PICTURE OF YOUR FAVORITE DINOSAUR HERE:

WELCOME!

If you love dinosaurs and enjoy activities, you're in the right place! This book is filled with fun dinosaur activities to do and dinosaur pictures to color. You will learn lots of interesting facts about dinosaurs while doing word search puzzles, mazes, dot-to-dots, and more!

WHEN DID DINOSAURS LIVE?

Dinosaurs lived between 252 and 145 million years ago during the Mesozoic Era. This era is divided into the Triassic, Jurassic, and Cretaceous periods. Different dinosaurs lived during each period. Color the dinosaurs below!

MESOZOIC ERA		
TRIASSIC 252 to 201 million years ago	**JURASSIC** 201 to 145 million years ago	**CRETACEOUS** 145 to 66 million years ago

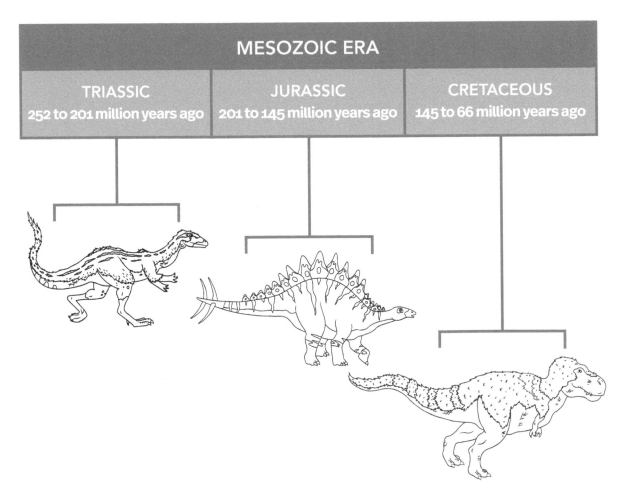

ALL ABOUT
MY FAVORITE DINOSAUR AND ME

My name is _____. I am _____ years old.

I love dinosaurs because _____

_____ .

My favorite dinosaur is _____

because _____ .

If I could dig for dinosaur fossils, I would travel to _____

_____ .

If I lived in prehistoric times, I would like to _____

_____ .

If dinosaurs could talk, I would ask them _____

_____ .

If I had a dinosaur as a pet, I would name it _____ .

My favorite thing to do with my dinosaur would be _____

_____ .

My favorite book to read to my dinosaur would be _____

_____ by _____ .

My dinosaur's favorite treat would be _____ .

TOOTHY T-REX

Tyrannosaurus rex (tie-RAN-oh-SAWR-us REX) had very sharp teeth and strong jaws. It could swallow 110 pounds of meat in one bite! Find the 5 things hidden in the picture.

moth   leaf   two ants   mushroom

Answer Key: page 76

ESCAPE THE VOLCANO

Tyrannosaurus rex was the largest carnivore (meat eater) to ever live in North America. Help this *Tyrannosaurus rex* find its way through the maze to escape erupting volcanoes!

Answer Key: page 76

FABULOUS FEATURES

Archaeopteryx (ar-key-OP-tur-icks) was a small carnivore. It had features of both dinosaurs and birds! Scientists think it was the earliest bird. The words in the puzzle are some of its features. Can you find these 5 words hidden in the puzzle? Words are hidden left to right and up to down.

TEETH   CLAWS   TAIL

FEATHERS   WINGS

Q F Y M T K J R

B E L G T O W Z

M A K W I N G S

T T C V V J O V

E H P Z T F W P

E E C L A W S T

T R R B I X L B

H S W M L N P K

CLIMB AND GLIDE

Archaeopteryx climbed trees using its claws.
It could jump and glide from tree to tree.

FINDING FISH

Elasmosaurus (ee-LAZ-mo-SAWR-us) swam in the open ocean. It fed on fish. Help this *Elasmosaurus* find its way through the maze to get fish.

Answer Key: page 76

SLOW SWIMMER

The slow-swimming *Elasmosaurus* had a very long neck. It had four flippers instead of arms and legs.

PADDLE TAIL

Spinosaurus (SPINE-oh-SAWR-us) had a jaw like a crocodile.
Its long tail worked like a paddle as it swam in the water.
Connect the dots to reveal this dinosaur's long tail.

Answer Key: page 76

TERRIFIC TOOLS

A paleontologist is a scientist who studies fossils to learn about life a long time ago. The following words are some of the tools that a paleontologist uses to dig up dinosaur bones. Can you find these 5 words hidden in the puzzle? Words are hidden left to right and up to down.

HAMMER   PICK   SHOVEL

CHISEL   BRUSH

```
C  Q  T  I  I  H  J
H  Y  B  O  V  A  R
I  P  I  C  K  M  O
S  L  H  R  Z  M  Y
E  S  H  O  V  E  L
L  E  I  F  V  R  X
L  B  R  U  S  H  Y
```

Answer Key: page 76

15

FINDING FOSSILS

This paleontologist has found some fossils! She will dig them up carefully.

ALL THE FRILLS

Triceratops (try-SEH-rah-tops) was a heavy herbivore (plant eater). It had three horns. It also had a large, bony collar called a frill to protect its neck. Connect the dots to form the frill for this *Triceratops*.

TASTY TREATS

This *Triceratops* herd is enjoying a meal of ferns and old logs.

THUMBS-UP

Iguanodon (ig-WAHN-oh-don) was a large herbivore. It lived in herds. It had sharp spikes on its thumbs that were used for protection or to help grasp food. Can you spot the 5 differences between these pictures?

HAPPY HATCHLINGS

These dinosaur eggs are hatching! Draw some baby dinosaurs in the nest.

DOT-TO-DOT DIPLODOCUS

Diplodocus (di-PLOH-duh-kus) was one of the longest dinosaurs. It was over 80 feet long. That is nearly as long as two school buses! Connect the dots to draw *Diplodocus*.

FLYING HOME

Many people think *Pteranodon* (ta-RAN-oh-don) was a dinosaur, but it was not. It was a flying reptile! It soared over the ocean looking for fish to scoop up with its long beak. Help this *Pteranodon* through the maze to reach its home.

Answer Key: page 77

FIND IT IN THE FLOCK

Pteranodon had a large crest on its head. Its wingspan was 12 to 18 feet wide! It lived in huge flocks. Find the 6 things hidden in the picture.

fish   flower   dragonfly

fern   seashell   bone

Answer Key: page 77

MIXED-UP MOSASAURUS

Mosasaurus (mo-sa-SAWR-us) was a reptile that lived in the water. But it breathed air and gave birth to live young like a mammal. Can you spot the 5 differences between these pictures?

Answer Key: page 77

MOSASAURUS MUNCHIES

Mosasaurus was a powerful swimmer. It used its paddle-like flippers to steer. The words in the puzzle are some of the things it ate. Can you find these 5 words hidden in the puzzle? Words are hidden left to right, up to down, and diagonally left to right.

FISH   CRAB   SEABIRD

TURTLE   SQUID

```
T  U  R  T  L  E  T  D  S  J
L  R  L  W  Q  Z  C  J  Q  Q
S  S  E  A  B  I  R  D  W  A
Q  Q  V  G  W  J  B  M  V  N
N  F  U  U  T  L  O  K  V  W
B  X  D  I  T  O  D  C  G  F
Y  P  P  J  D  B  Z  R  A  I
W  B  W  U  Q  C  C  A  I  S
J  U  X  O  U  O  L  B  V  H
R  S  R  Z  Q  P  N  F  H  N
```

Answer Key: page 77

SPIKY STYRACOSAURUS

Styracosaurus (sty-RAK-o-SAWR-us) had a large frill with long spikes on it. It had small horns over its eyes and a long horn on its nose. Connect the dots to see why this dinosaur's name means "spiked lizard."

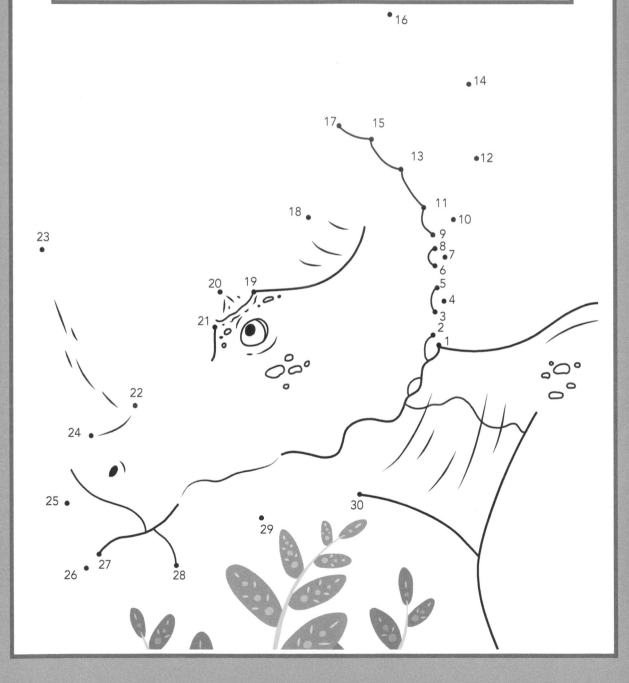

Answer Key: page 77

CHEW CHEW

Styracosaurus used its strong beak and many teeth to chew tough prehistoric plants.

SLOW AND STEADY

Stegosaurus (STEG-oh-SAWR-us) was a heavy, slow-moving herbivore.
It had large, bony plates on its back. Help this *Stegosaurus* find its way
through the forest for a tasty meal of ferns.

Answer Key: page 77

BONY PLATES

The bony plates along *Stegosaurus*'s spine could be as tall as a yardstick! Connect the dots to see the diamond-shaped plates on its back.

DINOSAUR TIME

Not all dinosaurs lived at the same time. Some had died out before others even appeared. When all the members of a species die out, that species is extinct. Can you find these 6 words hidden in the puzzle? Words are hidden left to right, up to down, and diagonally left to right.

MESOZOIC   TRIASSIC   CRETACEOUS

ERA   JURASSIC   EXTINCT

C T P D H B P Q J N

V R Q K J F O P Y O

A I E W U H R R D E

S A I T R H Z C S X

O S I J A D D Y U T

Y S F M S C C T X I

N I O Q S I E U N N

B C I U I O R O S C

E R A Z C E P G U T

L M E S O Z O I C S

Answer Key: page 77

CRETACEOUS COLORING

Many well-known dinosaurs, such as *Triceratops*, *Velociraptor*, and *Tyrannosaurus rex*, lived during the Cretaceous period.

DOME DINO

Pachycephalosaurus (pak-ee-SEF-uh-lo-SAWR-us) means "thick-headed lizard." They're known for their dome-shaped skulls. Connect the dots to complete the picture of *Pachycephalosaurus*.

Answer Key: page 77

WATCH YOUR HEAD!

The dome of a *Pachycephalosaurus* skull could be 10 inches thick! They probably used their heads to ram into each other when they fought over mates or territory.

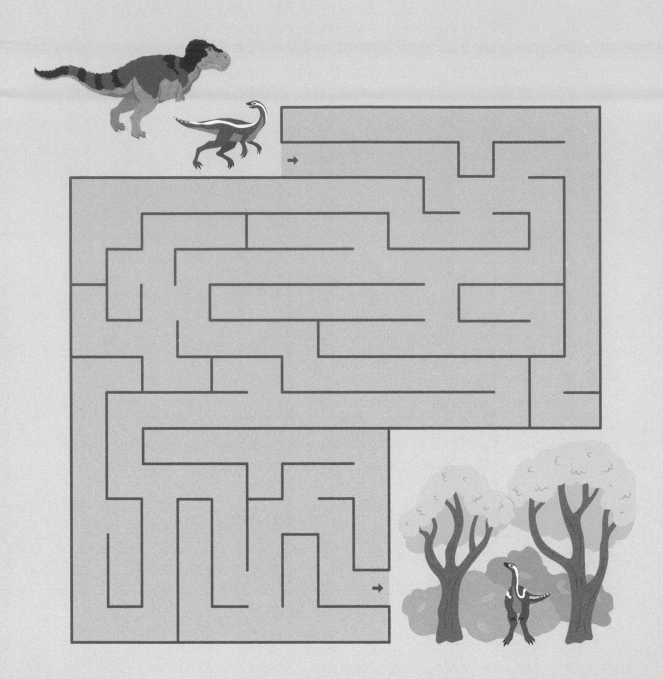

GO, GALLIMIMUS, GO!

Gallimimus (ga-luh-MY-mus) was one of the fastest dinosaurs. It could run up to 30 miles per hour. Help this *Gallimimus* sprint through the maze to get away from the predator.

Answer Key: page 78

GULP!

Gallimimus used its bird-like beak to eat small reptiles, insects, and eggs. It had no teeth. It swallowed its food whole. It lived in a herd for protection from predators.

SCARY-SAURUS

Ceratosaurus (KEH-rah-toh-SAWR-us) was a scary-looking dinosaur. It had a horn over each eye, razor-sharp teeth, and bony plates on its back. Can you find these 7 words hidden in the puzzle? Words are hidden left to right, up to down, and diagonally left to right.

BLADE   TEETH   SCARY

HORN   CLAWS

SHARP   PLATES

```
S  H  A  R  P  Y  H  X  J  N
F  W  W  W  U  N  V  O  Z  W
P  S  I  K  E  I  U  U  R  G
Z  L  H  Q  V  E  C  K  E  N
Z  I  A  M  M  K  L  Q  W  L
H  W  U  T  U  R  A  B  O  W
Y  V  K  D  E  L  W  L  W  Z
T  E  E  T  H  S  S  A  B  U
L  X  D  Q  C  P  P  D  V  O
N  S  C  A  R  Y  Y  E  V  N
```

Answer Key: page 78

36

CERATOSAURUS THE SHOW-OFF

Ceratosaurus means "horned lizard." This dinosaur probably used its horns to show off. Can you spot the 6 differences between these pictures?

Answer Key: page 78

FAMILY TIME

Lambeosaurus (LAM-bee-uh-SAWR-us) was a duck-billed dinosaur. It had a large, bony crest on top of its head. It traveled in herds. This protected the herd's babies from predators.

LAMBE'S LIZARD

Lambeosaurus is named after Lawrence Lambe. He was a Canadian paleontologist. The crest on its head looked like a hatchet with a handle-like bone sticking out the back. Connect the dots to see what it looked like!

FLYING REPTILES

Pterodactylus (tare-o-DACK-tull-us) was the first *pterosaur* (TEH-ruh-sor) ever discovered. This flying reptile had a wing-span of about three feet. It lived among the dinosaurs. Draw another *Pterodactylus* flying over the ocean looking for food.

SOMETHING'S FISHY

Pterodactylus has caught a fish. It is enjoying its meal on the beach. Find the 7 things hidden in the picture.

pine cone

butterfly

seed

twig

two feathers

horseshoe crab

Answer Key: page 78

HELMET HEAD

Corythosaurus (ko-rith-oh-SAWR-us) was a plant-eating, duck-billed dinosaur. It was between 30 and 33 feet long and weighed three to five tons. Its name means "helmet lizard." The bony crest on its head looked like a helmet!

CORYTHOSAURUS CALL

Corythosaurus could blow air through the hollow crest on its head. It sounded like a trumpet! This mother *Corythosaurus* is trumpeting to call her baby. Help the baby *Corythosaurus* find its way through the swamp maze to reach its mother.

Answer Key: page 78

SUPER DUPER

Supersaurus (SOO-per-SAWR-us) is one of the largest dinosaurs ever discovered. It was as long as a blue whale, the biggest animal on Earth today. *Supersaurus*'s neck was 40 feet long. That is as tall as 10 kids standing on top of each other! Connect the dots to reveal its neck.

Answer Key: page 78

SLOW SUPERSAURUS

Scientists think these "super lizards" lived in herds. They walked slowly. Their front feet looked like mittens. Their back feet looked like elephant feet.

TIME TO EAT

Some dinosaurs were herbivores. They ate only plants, like leaves, ferns, mosses, and cycad plants. Some dinosaurs were carnivores. They ate only meat, like other dinosaurs, lizards, turtles, and eggs. Others were omnivores. They ate both plants and animals. Can you find these 8 words hidden in the puzzle? Words are hidden left to right, right to left, top to bottom, and bottom to top.

LEAVES	CYCADS	TURTLES
FERNS	DINOSAURS	EGGS
MOSSES	LIZARDS	

```
N  H  E  M  M  O  S  S  E  S
L  F  C  Y  C  A  D  S  L  L
A  P  J  T  U  R  T  L  E  S
V  I  L  N  D  P  T  Z  Y  C
M  D  I  N  O  S  A  U  R  S
F  F  Z  S  E  V  A  E  L  I
I  E  A  O  S  O  T  O  B  E
W  R  R  T  G  N  A  A  Q  F
G  N  D  G  G  F  X  J  L  F
T  S  S  P  E  Z  W  A  X  J
```

Answer Key: page 78

SNACKING ON NUTS

Psittacosaurus (SIT-uh-ko-SAWR-us) used its strong parrot-like beak to crack open tough nuts for a snack. Draw some nut trees for this group of dinosaurs.

SPEEDY RAPTOR

Velociraptor (vuh-LAH-suh-RAP-tor) had hollow bones and feathers like a bird. But it did not fly. It was a carnivore that ran fast and hunted in packs. Can you spot the 7 differences between these pictures?

Answer Key: page 78

KILLING CLAW

Velociraptor had a large, curved claw on the second toe of each foot. Scientists call it the "killing claw." The claw hooked prey and kept it from escaping. Connect the dots to see the *Velociraptor*'s fierce claw.

Answer Key: page 79

EYE SEE YOU

Coelophysis (see-loe-FYE-sees) was a small, fast carnivore. It lived in what is now Arizona and Mexico. It had a long, narrow head and excellent eyesight. It could see as well as modern birds of prey, like hawks and eagles.

SPACE DINO

Coelophysis went to space! In 1998, a *Coelophysis* skull was taken aboard the space shuttle *Endeavor*. It went to the *Mir* space station. Find the 7 things hidden in the picture.

watch   stars   comb   book

rock   paper clip   pencil

Answer Key: page 79

WHAT A LONG NECK!

Brachiosaurus (BRACK-ee-oh-SAWR-us) was one of the tallest creatures to ever live on Earth. This giraffe-like dinosaur had a very long neck. Its front legs were longer than its back legs.

EAT YOUR VEGETABLES

Because of its size, *Brachiosaurus* had to eat between 400 and 800 pounds of plants each day! Help this *Brachiosaurus* find its way through the maze to the forest.

Answer Key: page 79

ARMORED TANK

Ankylosaurus (ANG-kee-lo-SAWR-us) was a plant-eating dinosaur. Its body was covered with an armor of thick, bony plates called scutes. These are similar to what we see on turtles and crocodiles today.

CLUB TAIL

The armor of the *Ankylosaurus* protected it from predators like the *Tyrannosaurus rex*. *Ankylosaurus* also had a strong tail with a bony mass at the end. It could swing its tail like a club to shatter the bones of another dinosaur. Can you find these 8 words hidden in the puzzle? Words are hidden left to right, right to left, top to bottom, and bottom to top.

STRONG   CLUB   THICK

BONY   TAIL   SCUTES

PLATES   ARMOR

```
C  L  U  B  X  J  C  M  T  T
A  V  C  H  S  C  U  T  E  S
R  C  C  C  D  B  J  S  K  P
M  M  Y  N  O  B  B  Y  C  J
O  P  L  A  T  E  S  G  I  B
R  F  Z  W  V  B  Y  N  H  N
C  D  O  V  S  E  E  O  T  Y
K  L  I  A  T  W  R  R  F  C
Y  T  N  A  N  S  R  T  B  T
P  L  B  R  S  V  B  S  X  U
```

Answer Key: page 79

DINOSAUR OR CROCODILE?

Suchomimus (SOOK-o-MY-mus) means "crocodile mimic." This large dinosaur had a head like a crocodile's. It had a narrow skull and a short neck. It had more than 100 teeth that curved backward. Connect the dots. See if you can tell which one is the dinosaur and which one is the crocodile!

Answer Key: page 79

CATCH SOME FISH

With its long snout and huge thumb claws, *Suchomimus* excelled at catching fish.

TERRIBLE LIZARDS

Many dinosaur names come from Greek words. In Greek, *deinos* means "terrible" and *sauros* means "lizard." So *dinosaur* means "terrible lizard." Can you find the 8 terrible lizards hidden in the puzzle? Words are hidden left to right, right to left, top to bottom, and bottom to top.

DINOSAUR

STEGOSAURUS

TRICERATOPS

ALLOSAURUS

VELOCIRAPTOR

MEGALOSAURUS

CORYTHOSAURUS

BARYONYX

```
A L L O S A U R U S Q K S O D
C D V R E C N L W I Z Q P K F
S T O G I O U T M H U J O E G
I D N P S R G S X Z W C T O C
B V K E X Y N O Y R A B A N D
Y A I V I T U N P Q V P R U I
I P O T L H V V Z A H D E H N
M E G A L O S A U R U S C R O
L C O E F S N Z N P Y L I H S
V Q H W Y A P H S Y R J R D A
Q B U D Y U R M S J X T I U
I N P S U R U A S O G E T S R
C R A C E U E S B M Z K Q M F
W M B B P S G V L M F T R Z S
D R O T P A R I C O L E V D G
```

Answer Key: page 79

MIGHTY MEGALOSAURUS

Megalosaurus (MEG-uh-low-SAWR-us) was a large, strong carnivore. It would catch its own food or steal food from smaller carnivores. It had short arms with three clawed fingers. Draw some dinosaurs for the *Megalosaurus* to chase.

COLOR THE CAMARASAURUS

Camarasaurus (kuh-MARE-uh-SAWR-us) was a large herbivore. It had a skull shaped like an arch. It also had air sacs in the bones of its spine. The air sacs helped it breathe.

DIGGING FOR FOSSILS

Camarasaurus is the most commonly found dinosaur in the Jurassic rocks of North America. Paleontologists have found many of their bones, including complete skeletons. Help this paleontologist through the maze so he can study the *Camarasaurus* bones.

Answer Key: page 79

IS THAT AN OSTRICH?

Ornithomimus (or-ni-thoh-MEE-mus) was a dinosaur that looked like an ostrich. It had a small toothless beak, long legs, and feathers. Like the ostrich, it did not fly, but it could run fast. *Ornithomimus* mostly ate plants, but it probably ate some insects and other small animals, too. This means it was an omnivore. Can you find these 8 words hidden in the puzzle? Words are hidden left to right, right to left, top to bottom, and bottom to top.

DINOSAUR   OSTRICH   RUN

TOOTHLESS   FEATHERS   LEGS

BEAK   OMNIVORE

```
A T L F V P D W O K W I J
Q B T K F V U D Y O I R E
Y T A F E T B I K Z I A R
V A C L A R V N I V T Q U
D P E X T N I O D N I L X
G T Y S H Z H S C H M E L
N J O B E A K A L C O G A
E D Q X R D R U N I N S F
P X Q N S J W R Z R X A G
T O O T H L E S S T T H P
A Q N V O A N O B S L E G
V K Z E O M N I V O R E E
A Z W G Z K J M H H K X N
```

Answer Key: page 79

OBSERVE THE ORNITHOMIMUS

Ornithomimus had three toes that it used to dig in the ground. It could run about 30 miles per hour! Find the 8 things hidden in the picture.

	butterfly		worm		bone		dinosaur poop
	berry		fish		beetle		dinosaur egg

Answer Key: page 79

CALL ME SPIKE

Stygimoloch (STIJ-i-MOL-ock) was a small herbivore. It walked on two legs. This odd-looking dinosaur had spikes and bumps on its head. Paleontologists now think *Stygimoloch* was actually a young *Pachycephalosaurus*.

BUILD THE BARYONYX

Baryonyx (BARE-ee-ON-icks) was a medium-size carnivore. It ate fish. It walked on two legs and had long claws. Its long snout had 95 teeth! It was closely related to *Spinosaurus*, but it did not have the large sail on its back. Connect the dots to see *Baryonyx*.

Answer Key: page 80

FISHING LIKE A BEAR

Baryonyx hunted much like a grizzly bear does. It crouched on riverbanks or waded in shallow water to grab fish with its cone-shaped teeth. Help the *Baryonyx* reach the stream to catch the fish.

Answer Key: page 80

AWESOME ALLOSAURUS

Allosaurus (AL-oh-SAWR-us) was one of the deadliest carnivores in North America. It was a top predator during the Jurassic period. It looked like a smaller *Tyrannosaurus rex*.

FAST FOOD

Allosaurus could run up to 20 miles per hour. It used its powerful arms and sharp claws to catch and hold on to its prey. It bit off chunks of meat with its strong teeth and jaws. Can you spot the 8 differences between these pictures?

Answer Key: page 80

PIPE HEAD

Parasaurolophus (pa-ra-SAWR-oh-LOAF-us) was an herbivore. It had an unusual crest that formed a long, curved pipe on the back of its head. It could blow through this crest and make a sound like a musical instrument! Connect the dots to see *Parasaurolophus*.

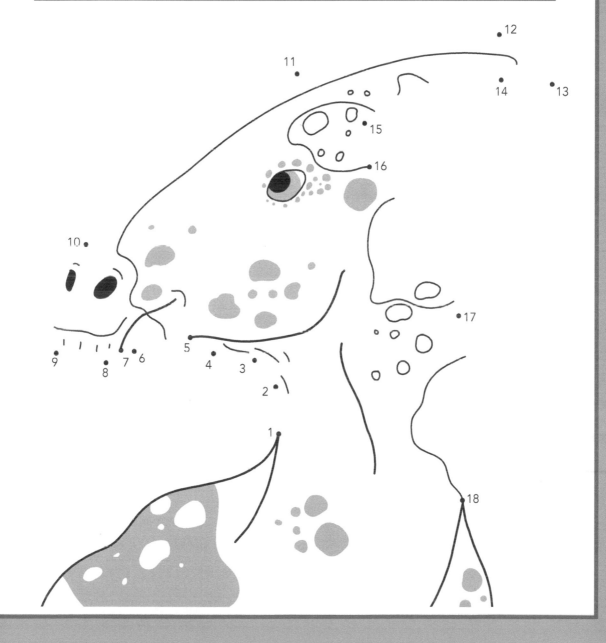

REACH UP HIGH

Parasaurolophus walked on four legs. It could also stand on its back legs to reach high for food. Help this *Parasaurolophus* through the maze to find its herd.

Answer Key: page 80

BULL HORNS

Carnotaurus (CAR-no-TAW-rus) means "meat-eating bull." Like a bull, *Carnotaurus* had large horns on its head. It had very short, weak arms. It used its powerful horns to knock down prey.

CARNIVOROUS CARNOTAURUS

Carnotaurus was a carnivore with over 50 small but powerful teeth. This *Carnotaurus* is missing its horns and teeth! Can you draw them in?

WHERE DID ALL THE DINOSAURS GO?

Many dinosaurs—except birds!—died out about 66 million years ago. There were many theories, or guesses, about what happened. Some people used to think a huge volcano erupted or diseases wiped them out. Scientists now think that a giant piece of rock from space called an asteroid struck Earth. This caused many different animals to die off. When the last of a species dies, that species is extinct. Can you find these 8 words about dinosaur extinction hidden in the puzzle? Words are hidden right to left, bottom to top, diagonally right to left, and diagonally left to right.

EXTINCT   THEORY   SPECIES   ERUPT

SCIENTISTS   ASTEROID   VOLCANO   DISEASE

```
E S A E S I D T F S X W F P P
L S M M V B F G C R H R Y O F
F L E K H D S I F O Z K E P B
S A H L H E E Q L W W X A B N
B K I R V N N C G H T Q T U X
I D K D T O M I H I H Y P N H
X Z I I A M L I N A H F U X L
D C S O G A D C R J G C R C E
X T D B R Y T A A U B S E J S
S U V I X E X M W N L R M E E
Q H G F O X T P A M O X I G J
U D M M E Z Q S N Z H C E B L
D I D Q G I K P A E E I K L V
N V G Z T G T H A P C Z E K Z
G U Y R O E H T S E P X Z Z J
```

Answer Key: page 80

DINOSAUR DISCOVERY

You have discovered a new dinosaur. Now you get to name it! Draw a picture of what it looks like. Write its name.

_____

ANSWER KEY

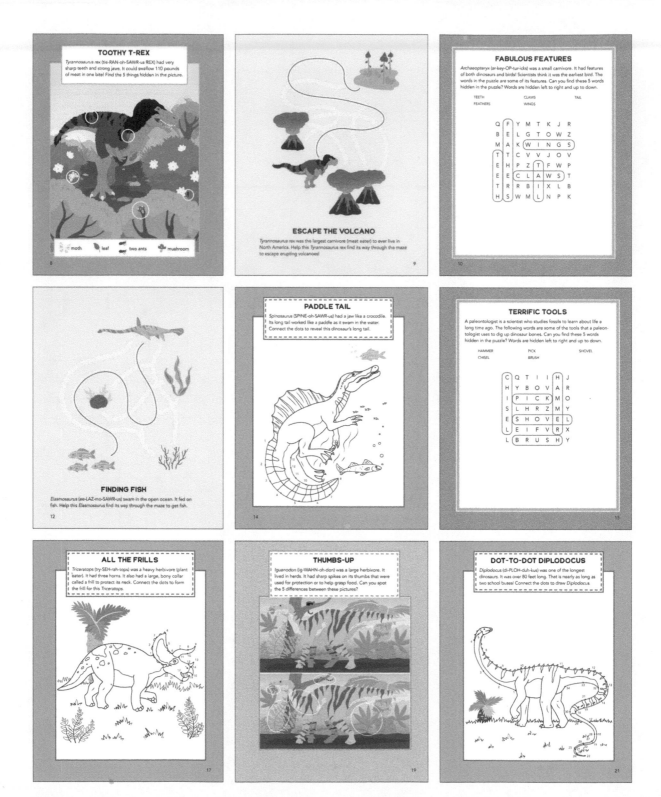

TOOTHY T-REX

Tyrannosaurus rex (tie-RAN-oh-SAWR-us REX) had very sharp teeth and strong jaws. It could swallow 110 pounds of meat in one bite! Find the 5 things hidden in the picture.

moth   leaf   two ants   mushroom

8

ESCAPE THE VOLCANO

Tyrannosaurus rex was the largest carnivore (meat eater) to ever live in North America. Help this Tyrannosaurus rex find its way through the maze to escape erupting volcanoes!

9

FABULOUS FEATURES

Archaeopteryx (ar-key-OP-tur-icks) was a small carnivore. It had features of both dinosaurs and birds! Scientists think it was the earliest bird. The words in the puzzle are some of its features. Can you find these 5 words hidden in the puzzle? Words are hidden left to right and up to down.

TEETH   CLAWS   TAIL
FEATHERS   WINGS

10

FINDING FISH

Elasmosaurus (ee-LAZ-mo-SAWR-us) swam in the open ocean. It fed on fish. Help this Elasmosaurus find its way through the maze to get fish.

12

PADDLE TAIL

Spinosaurus (SPINE-oh-SAWR-us) had a jaw like a crocodile. Its long tail worked like a paddle as it swam in the water. Connect the dots to reveal this dinosaur's long tail.

14

TERRIFIC TOOLS

A paleontologist is a scientist who studies fossils to learn about life a long time ago. The following words are some of the tools that a paleontologist uses to dig up dinosaur bones. Can you find these 5 words hidden in the puzzle? Words are hidden left to right and up to down.

HAMMER   PICK   SHOVEL
CHISEL   BRUSH

15

ALL THE FRILLS

Triceratops (try-SEH-rah-tops) was a heavy herbivore (plant eater). It had three horns. It also had a large, bony collar called a frill to protect its neck. Connect the dots to form the frill for this Triceratops.

17

THUMBS-UP

Iguanodon (ig-WAHN-oh-don) was a large herbivore. It lived in herds. It had sharp spikes on its thumbs that were used for protection or to help grasp food. Can you spot the 5 differences between these pictures?

19

DOT-TO-DOT DIPLODOCUS

Diplodocus (di-PLOH-duh-kus) was one of the longest dinosaurs. It was over 80 feet long. That is nearly as long as two school buses! Connect the dots to draw Diplodocus.

21

ANSWER KEY

FLYING HOME

Many people think *Pteranodon* (ta-RAN-oh-don) was a dinosaur, but it was not. It was a flying reptile! It soared over the ocean looking for fish to scoop up with its long beak. Help this *Pteranodon* through the maze to reach its home.

22

FIND IT IN THE FLOCK

Pteranodon had a large crest on its head. Its wingspan was 12 to 18 feet wide! It lived in huge flocks. Find the 6 things hidden in the picture.

fish   flower   dragonfly
fern   seashell   bone

23

MIXED-UP MOSASAURUS

Mosasaurus (mo-sa-SAWR-us) was a reptile that lived in the water. But it breathed air and gave birth to live young like a mammal. Can you spot the 5 differences between these pictures?

26

MOSASAURUS MUNCHIES

Mosasaurus was a powerful swimmer. It used its paddle-like flippers to steer. The words in the puzzle are some of the things it ate. Can you find these 5 words hidden in the puzzle? Words are hidden left to right, up to down, and diagonally left to right.

FISH   CRAB   SEABIRD
TURTLE   SQUID

T	U	R	T	L	E	T	D	S	J
L	R	L	W	Q	Z	C	J	Q	Q
S	S	E	A	B	I	R	D	W	A
Q	Q	V	G	W	J	B	M	V	N
N	F	U	U	T	L	O	K	V	W
B	X	D	I	T	O	D	C	G	F
Y	P	J	D	B	Z	R	A	I	I
W	B	W	U	Q	C	C	A	B	S
J	U	X	O	U	O	L	B	V	H
R	S	R	Z	Q	P	N	F	H	N

25

SPIKY STYRACOSAURUS

Styracosaurus (sty-RAK-o-SAWR-us) had a large frill with long spikes on it. It had small horns over its eyes and a long horn on its nose. Connect the dots to see why this dinosaur's name means "spiked lizard."

26

SLOW AND STEADY

Stegosaurus (STEG-oh-SAWR-us) was a heavy, slow-moving herbivore. It had large, bony plates on its back. Help this *Stegosaurus* find its way through the forest for a tasty meal of ferns.

28

BONY PLATES

The bony plates along *Stegosaurus's* spine could be as tall as a yardstick! Connect the dots to see the diamond-shaped plates on its back.

29

DINOSAUR TIME

Not all dinosaurs lived at the same time. Some had died out before others even appeared. When all the members of a species die out, that species is extinct. Can you find these 6 words hidden in the puzzle? Words are hidden left to right, up to down, and diagonally left to right.

MESOZOIC   TRIASSIC   CRETACEOUS
ERA   JURASSIC   EXTINCT

C	T	P	D	H	B	P	Q	J	N
R	Q	K	J	F	O	P	Y	O	
A	I	E	W	U	H	R	R	D	E
S	S	I	T	H	Z	C	S	X	
O	S	I	J	A	D	Y	U	T	
Y	S	F	M	S	C	C	T	X	I
N	I	U	Q	S	I	E	U	N	
B	C	I	U	I	O	R	O	S	C
E	R	A	Z	C	E	P	G	U	T
L	M	E	S	O	Z	O	I	C	S

30

DOME DINO

Pachycephalosaurus (pak-ee-SEF-uh-lo-SAWR-us) means "thick-headed lizard." They're known for their dome-shaped skulls. Connect the dots to complete the picture of *Pachycephalosaurus*.

32

77

ANSWER KEY

ANSWER KEY

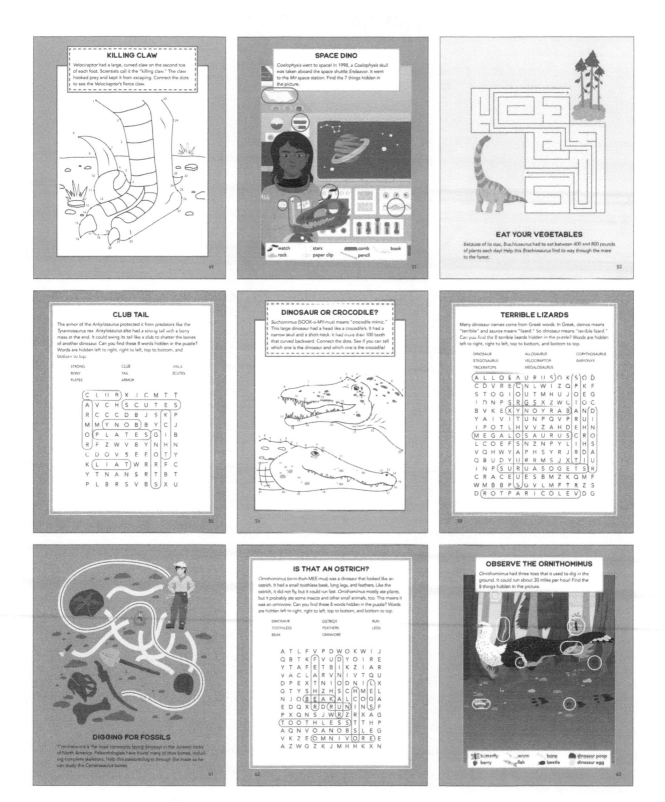

KILLING CLAW

Velociraptor had a large, curved claw on the second toe of each foot. Scientists call it the "killing claw." The claw hooked prey and kept it from escaping. Connect the dots to see the *Velociraptor's* fierce claw.

49

SPACE DINO

Coelophysis went to space! In 1998, a *Coelophysis* skull was taken aboard the space shuttle *Endeavor*. It went to the *Mir* space station. Find the 7 things hidden in the picture.

watch • stars • comb • book • rock • paper clip • pencil

51

EAT YOUR VEGETABLES

Because of its size, *Brachiosaurus* had to eat between 400 and 800 pounds of plants each day! Help this *Brachiosaurus* find its way through the maze to the forest.

53

CLUB TAIL

The armor of the *Ankylosaurus* protected it from predators like the *Tyrannosaurus rex*. *Ankylosaurus* also had a strong tail with a bony mass at the end. It could swing its tail like a club to shatter the bones of another dinosaur. Can you find these 8 words hidden in the puzzle? Words are hidden left to right, right to left, top to bottom, and bottom to top.

STRONG • CLUB • TAIL
BONY • TAIL • SCUTES
PLATES • ARMOR

55

DINOSAUR OR CROCODILE?

Suchomimus (SOOK-o-MY-mus) means "crocodile mimic." This large dinosaur had a head like a crocodile's. It had a narrow skull and a short neck. It had more than 100 teeth that curved backward. Connect the dots. See if you can tell which one is the dinosaur and which one is the crocodile!

56

TERRIBLE LIZARDS

Many dinosaur names come from Greek words. In Greek, *deinos* means "terrible" and *sauros* means "lizard." So dinosaur means "terrible lizard." Can you find the 8 terrible lizards hidden in the puzzle? Words are hidden left to right, right to left, top to bottom, and bottom to top.

DINOSAUR • ALLOSAURUS • CORYTHOSAURUS
STEGOSAURUS • VELOCIRAPTOR • BARYONYX
TRICERATOPS • MEGALOSAURUS

58

DIGGING FOR FOSSILS

Camarasaurus is the most commonly found dinosaur in the Jurassic rocks of North America. Paleontologists have found many of their bones, including complete skeletons. Help this paleontologist through the maze so he can study the *Camarasaurus* bones.

61

IS THAT AN OSTRICH?

Ornithomimus (or-ni-thoh-MEE-mus) was a dinosaur that looked like an ostrich. It had a small toothless beak, long legs, and feathers. Like the ostrich, it did not fly, but it could run fast. *Ornithomimus* mostly ate plants, but it probably ate some insects and other small animals, too. This means it was an omnivore. Can you find these 8 words hidden in the puzzle? Words are hidden left to right, right to left, top to bottom, and bottom to top.

DINOSAUR • OSTRICH • RUN
TOOTHLESS • FEATHERS • LEGS
BEAK • OMNIVORE

62

OBSERVE THE ORNITHOMIMUS

Ornithomimus had three toes that it used to dig in the ground. It could run about 30 miles per hour! Find the 8 things hidden in the picture.

butterfly • worm • bone • dinosaur poop
berry • fish • beetle • dinosaur egg

63

79

ANSWER KEY

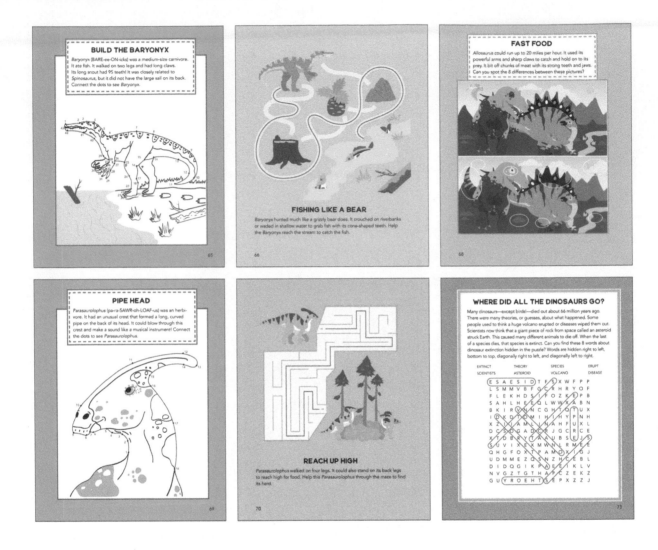

BUILD THE BARYONYX

Baryonyx (BARE-ee-ON-icks) was a medium-size carnivore. It ate fish. It walked on two legs and had long claws. Its long snout had 95 teeth! It was closely related to *Spinosaurus*, but it did not have the large sail on its back. Connect the dots to see *Baryonyx*.

65

FISHING LIKE A BEAR

Baryonyx hunted much like a grizzly bear does. It crouched on riverbanks or waded in shallow water to grab fish with its cone-shaped teeth. Help the *Baryonyx* reach the stream to catch the fish.

66

FAST FOOD

Allosaurus could run up to 20 miles per hour. It used its powerful arms and sharp claws to catch and hold on to its prey. It bit off chunks of meat with its strong teeth and jaws. Can you spot the 8 differences between these pictures?

68

PIPE HEAD

Parasaurolophus (pa-ra-SAWR-oh-LOAF-us) was an herbivore. It had an unusual crest that formed a long, curved pipe on the back of its head. It could blow through this crest and make a sound like a musical instrument! Connect the dots to see *Parasaurolophus*.

69

REACH UP HIGH

Parasaurolophus walked on four legs. It could also stand on its back legs to reach high for food. Help this *Parasaurolophus* through the maze to find its herd.

70

WHERE DID ALL THE DINOSAURS GO?

Many dinosaurs—except birds!—died out about 66 million years ago. There were many theories, or guesses, about what happened. Some people used to think a huge volcano erupted or diseases wiped them out. Scientists now think that a giant piece of rock from space called an asteroid struck Earth. This caused many different animals to die off. When the last of a species dies, that species is extinct. Can you find these 8 words about dinosaur extinction hidden in the puzzle? Words are hidden right to left, bottom to top, diagonally right to left, and diagonally left to right.

EXTINCT   THEORY   SPECIES   ERUPT
SCIENTISTS   ASTEROID   VOLCANO   DISEASE

73

ABOUT THE AUTHOR

 **Lauren Thompson** earned her BS in interdisciplinary studies with an early childhood certification from Texas A&M University–Commerce. She taught third grade in Texas before moving overseas with her family. She spent almost 10 years in the Middle East partnering with nonprofit organizations while homeschooling her five children. She started her website Mrs. Thompson's Treasures (MrsThompsonsTreasures.com) as a way to share fun and engaging resources for elementary school teachers and parents. Lauren currently lives with her family in Texas and loves traveling, reading, and drinking lots of coffee.

ABOUT THE ILLUSTRATOR

Sara Lynn Cramb illustrates educational books for kids. She has created illustrations for many titles including *Search the Ocean Find the Animals, Animals of the World: A Lift-the-Flap Book*, and *If You Are a Kaka, You Eat Doo Doo*. Sara loves creating work that excites and educates kids about the natural world, including the prehistoric world. *Triceratops* is her favorite dinosaur and has been so since childhood. She currently lives in Fairbanks, Alaska with her partner, two grumpy turtles, and a pair of mischievous cats.

Printed in the USA
CPSIA information can be obtained
at www.ICGtesting.com
CBHW040711120324
5247CB00002B/3